Jaiza Sammara de Araujo Alves

Female Crime in Brazil and Argentina

Jaiza Sammara de Araujo Alves

Female Crime in Brazil and Argentina

A statistical study of women and crime in Brazil and Argentina

ScienciaScripts

Imprint

Cover image: www.ingimage.com

This book is a translation from the original published under ISBN 978-620-2-04580-3.

Publisher:
Sciencia Scripts
is a trademark of
Dodo Books Indian Ocean Ltd. and OmniScriptum S.R.L publishing group

120 High Road, East Finchley, London, N2 9ED, United Kingdom
Str. Armeneasca 28/1, office 1, Chisinau MD-2012, Republic of Moldova, Europe
Managing Directors: Ieva Konstantinova, Victoria Ursu
info@omniscriptum.com

Printed at: see last page
ISBN: 978-620-8-53783-8

Female criminality:
A Descriptive Study of Statistical Data on Women in Detention in Brazil and Argentina

Jaiza Sammara de Araujo Alves

PhD student in Criminal Law at the Universidad de Buenos Aires; specialist in Criminal Law and Criminal Procedure at Uniseb/Praetorium; specialist in Legal Psychology at the Faculdade de Ciencias Aplicadas e Sociais de Petrolina - PE (Facape); specialist in Business Law at the Universidade Regional do Cariri (Urca); professor of Criminal Law II at Facape; coordinator of Facape's Jury Practice Center. jaizasam@yahoo.com.br

Summary

The purpose of this article is to investigate the profile of women who are imprisoned in Brazil and Argentina, analyzing their socio-economic conditions. Initially, an analysis will be made of female inferiority through history, as well as female criminality, which for a long time has been disregarded by legal operators. Finally, a study will be made of the statistical data collected in both countries, in order to observe the common and divergent characteristics of women who are detained for crimes in Brazil and Argentina.

Keywords: Women. Incarceration. Brazil. Argentina.

INTRODUCTION

Male supremacy has always been evident throughout human history, and in Greco-Roman antiquity women were seen only as speaking objects owned by their masters, be they fathers, brothers, husbands or sons, without even being considered subjects of rights. In other words, at that time, women were completely submissive to men, given that the sacred fire religion itself preached their inferiority to men, since there was no transmission of the sacred cult to descendants through the female lineage. Thus, "Greek, Roman and Hindu law, which originated from these religious beliefs, all agree that women are inferior".[1]

In the Middle Ages, in addition to being inferior, women were considered to be tempted by the devil, who could lead men to the loss not only of their bodies, but above all of their souls. The justification used at the time, also linked to religion, was that the woman (Eve) had been created from an irregular rib of the man (Adao) and was therefore imperfect, and that God would have preferred the man to the woman. In addition, women were considered evil and endowed with perversions due to original sin:

---

[1] COULANGES, Fustel de. *The Ancient City* - Studies in the Cult, Law and Institutions of Greece and Rome. 12. ed. translated by Jonas Camargo Leite and Eduardo Fonseca. Sao Paulo: Hemus, 1975. p. 69.

Se habla en *Eclesiasticus* XXV: No cabeza superior a la de una ser- piente, y no hay ira superior a la de una mujer. I prefer to live with a lion and a dragon than with a malevolent woman (...) all malignancies are nothing compared to that of a woman.[2]

This understanding of female inferiority was ratified in the book *Malleus Maleficarum* or Hammer of the Witches, a veritable compendium that taught how to recognize, prosecute and punish a witch. Thus, women who didn't fit into society's "normal" lifestyle were considered witches and, as a result, countless of them were killed in Inquisition bonfires because of the supposed power they possessed over people considered normal. In this way, women who fell outside social standards became criminalized, not because of their conduct, but because of what they represented, being considered a true enemy of everything that was good and moral, and therefore deserved to be eliminated from society. This same position of women's inferiority was corroborated centuries later by Lombroso and Ferrero in their book *The Delinquent Woman*. These authors stated that women occupied a lower position on the evolutionary scale and were not even capable of committing crimes; however, delinquent women resembled men and were

[2] KRAMER, Heinrich; SPRENGER, Jacobus. *Malleus Maleficarum*. Translated by Floreal Maza, 1486, p. 49.

therefore more likely to commit crimes. In this way, both authors, in the middle of the 19th century, were corroborating what had been said by Heinrich Kramer and Jacobus Sprenger in *Malleus Maleficarum*.

It should be noted that it was only in the 1970s that studies on female delinquency began to take on greater importance, since previously female inferiority dominated the thinking of even the majority of legal professionals, who preferred to hide the issue rather than discuss it. The same was (is) true of the penitentiary system, laws and penal execution, which, with the use of the terms "convict and internee", end up sending out a subliminal message that female criminality is irrelevant to the criminal justice system.

The aim of this article is therefore to look at female criminality, analyzing the profile of women who are imprisoned in Brazil and Argentina, especially in relation to their socio-economic status.

The work used bibliographical research, based on various Brazilian and foreign authors who are references in the field, as well as quantitative research, based on statistics from both countries, showing the numbers of female criminals in Brazil and Argentina, as well as drawing a picture of who the women detained in both nations are.

Initially, a historical analysis was made of the inferiority of women in relation to men, as well as an approach to female criminality. Subsequently, using data presented by Infopen,[3] in 2014, by Argentine institutes and other international institutes, the profiles of women who are incarcerated in Brazil and Argentina were studied, presenting recent figures on female crime in both countries, analyzing the main age group, level of education, marital status, among other points, seeking to investigate who the women are who are incarcerated in prisons in both countries, and whether there are common and divergent points between them.

[3] Statistical information system for the Brazilian penitentiary system.

1 FEMALE INFERIORITY IN HISTORY

Throughout human history, women have always been discriminated against and considered inferior to men. Moreover, for a long time they were seen as an object of male property, a being without capacity, weak and debilitated.

During Greco-Roman antiquity, the religion of the sacred fire was predominant, where people revered the dead ancestors as the main authority in the home. In second place was the authority of the *paterfamilias*, the father, head of the family, who was the first to the sacred fire, the one to whom the other members of the family owed obedience and respect. As for women, although they took part in the religious functions of the home, they did not enjoy a very high position and were not even the absolute masters of their own homes. This inferiority was due to the fact that the woman had not been born into that religion, since she had acquired it from her husband through marriage. Furthermore, she did not represent the ancestors, as she was not descended from them, and as soon as she died she would not receive a special cult either.[4] At that time, a woman would always be part of her husband, whether in life or in death.[5]

In this way, in Greco-Roman antiquity, women were

[4] COULANGES, Fustel de. *The Ancient City-studies* on the cult, the law, the institutes of Greece and Rome, op. cit. p. 69.
[5] Idem.

considered inferior and were always subordinated to male authority: as a mother, to her father; when her father died, to her brothers and relatives in the paternal line; when married, to her husband; if she was widowed, she remained submissive to her husband's subordinates (her husband's children or close relatives).[6] It should be noted that, at that time, female inferiority was also reflected in the sphere of criminal responsibility, since women were not punished for the crimes they committed, and it was up to the man to be held responsible for the criminal conduct. Thus, women were considered to be criminally irresponsible, and it was up to their closest relatives to be held responsible for their crimes.[7]

In the Middle Ages, with the rise of the dogmas of the Catholic Church, women were not only considered inferior to men, but also evil, capable of leading men astray, since if they did not resist temptation, they would be punished not only with the loss of their bodies, but mainly with the loss of their souls.[8] It should be noted that during the same period there was a belief that women were imperfect, because their bodies were disproportionate to those of men. Thus, since woman was

---

6 Idem.

7 LOBATO, Aline et al. *Women criminals:* analyzing the relationship between family breakdown and crime. p. 3. Available at: http://www.abrapso.org.br/siteprincipal/images/Anais_XVENABRAPSO/242.%20mulheres%20criminosas.pdfAccessed on: October 14, 2016.

8 BUENO DOMINGUEZ, Maria Luisa. La brujeria: los maleficios contra los hombres. In: *Clio y Crimen,* n. 8, p. 125-142, p. 130, 2011. Available at: <https://www.durango-udala.net/portalDurango/RecursosWeb/DOCUMENTOS/1/1_5142_3.pdf>. Accessed on: September 29, 2015.

created from an irregular rib of man, she was considered imperfect, and this imperfection also extended to her soul. It was even claimed that God had a predilection for man, placing woman on an inferior level. At the time, there was also a debate about whether women actually had souls, and if so, whether their souls lacked intellectual capacity, since they couldn't understand more complex things.[9] According to Otto Pollak, the belief that Eve was created from Adao's "crooked" rib justified the idea that women were more prone to lies, dissimulation and falsehood.[10]

This same position was defended by Heinrich Kramer and Jacob Sprenger in their book *Malleus Maleficarum* or Hammer of the Witches, written in1486. These authors claimed that women were weaker in body and mind and were therefore more easily influenced by witchcraft.[11] As a result, there were more witches than wizards and the aforementioned book was directly related to them: "The Witches".

It should be noted that the *Malleus Maleficarum* points out the characteristics of women who were considered witches:

---

[9] BUENO DOMINGUEZ, Maria Luisa. La brujeria: los maleficios contra los hombres. In: *Clio y Crimen,* n. 8, p. 125-142, p. 131, 2011. Available at: <https://www.durango-udala.net/portalDurango/RecursosWeb/DOCUMENTOS/1/1_5142_3.pdf>. Accessed on: September 29, 2015.

[10] POLLAK, Otto. *The criminality of women.* New York: Perpetua Books, 1961. p. 8.

[11] KRAMER, Heinrich; SPRENGER, Jacobus. *MalleusMaleficarum.* op. cit, p. 50.

ugly and deformed women, connected to the moon, since they practiced at night; the ability to fly on brooms or on animals.[12] Something that should be mentioned is that witches acted through the power of the devil, but everything was done with "God's permission". Thus, everything that was considered magical, strange, could be investigated by the inquisitors and the witch could be considered guilty, having to answer for her actions. It is important to note that women considered to be witches were often induced to confess their crimes, with the promise of not being sentenced to death, but this was a fallacy, a way for the inquisitor to extract a confession from the woman, with the latter being deceived as to the true intention of the inquisitor.[13][14][15][16] In this way, the confessed defendant was condemned to death for the crime of witchcraft, with the stake being the main form of execution. The intention, however, was not simply religious, since the real intention was to exclude women, a group that represented the majority at the time.

---

12 BUENO DOMINGUEZ, Maria Luisa. La brujeria: los maleficios contra los hombres. op. cit., p. 135.

13 PIRES, Joao Davi Avelar. The Inquisition and witchcraft: the ritualization of the interrogator and the torture. In: *Revista Historia e Cultura*, Franca, SP, v. 2, n. 3 (especial), p. 560-573, p. 563, 2013. Available at: <http://periodicos.franca.unesp.br/index.php/historiaecultura/arti-cle/view/1121>. Accessed on: September 29, 2015.

14 ANITUA, Gabriel Ignacio. *History of criminological thought.* Ciudad Autonoma de Buenos Aires: Ediciones Didot, 2015. p. 60.

15 ZAFFARONI, Eugenio Raul. *Women and punitive power.* 1992. Available at: <http://www.cubc.mx/biblioteca/libros/Zaffaroni%20-%20Mujer%20y%20poder%20punitivo.pdf>. Accessed on: September 28, 2015.

16 ANITUA, Gabriel Ignacio. *Historia de lospensamientos criminologicos.* op. cit., p. 63.

Thus, the decision to condemn witches to death was, in reality, political in nature, since "they" had great influence over the population and such "power" weakened the state and the Catholic Church.[14] Furthermore, by containing the "witches", the spread of paid religion was prevented,[15] favoring the growth of the influence of Christianity and its dogmas.

Later, with the rise of Absolutist states and their punitive power, the sanctions against witches became less cruel, since women were considered so inferior that they didn't even deserve to be punished for the crimes they had committed.[16]

In the 19th century, Lombroso wrote the book *The Delinquent Woman*, together with his son-in-law William Ferrero. This book affirms a return to inquisitorial ideas about female inferiority, considering women inferior even for committing crimes. It should be noted that the authors differentiate between "normal" women and criminal women and state that the former have greater cranial capacity than the latter, with prostitutes and criminals having lower cranial capacity than lunatics.[17] In addition, they claim that female criminals have flat heads,[18] abnormal teeth,[19] protruding

---

[17] LOMBROSO, Cesare; FERRERO, William. *The Female Offender*. New York: D. Appleton Company, 1898. p. 21.

[18] Ibid, p. 30.

[19] Idem.

jaws.[20] In addition, for the authors, women occupy a lower place on the evolutionary scale,[21] being conservative due to the static nature of the ovum in relation to the sperm.[22] In addition, men evolve more because they are less sedentary and are more exposed to varying conditions than women. So women are more primitive.[23] Lombroso and Ferrero cite certain characteristics of female criminals: "(...) in general, they do not feel pity and are therefore insensitive to the punishments of others, but they also acquire a lack of moral refinement that brings them closer to atavistic men".[24] Thus, for these authors, the few women delinquents are similar to men, and especially to ancestral men.[25] They are, however, more vicious than them, and there is a parallel between prostitution and delinquency. The authors, however, also differentiated male delinquency from female prostitution, considering the latter to be less harmful, perverse and terrible than the former. It should be noted that the authors affirmed the existence of a social function of prostitution, which functioned as a kind of escape valve for male sexuality, and could even prevent crimes from being committed,[26] such as sexual crimes in general and domestic

[20] Ibid, p. 33.

[21] ANITUA, Gabriel Ignacio. *Historia de lospensamientos criminologicos.* op. cit., p. 223.

[22] LOMBROSO, Cesare; FERRERO, William. *The female offender.* op. cit., p. 109.

[23] Idem.

[24] "In general, they don't feel pity and are therefore insensitive to the pity of others, and suffer from a lack of moral refinement that brings them closer to atavistic man." ANITUA, Gabriel Ignacio. *Historia de lospensamientos criminologicos.* op. cit., p. 223.

[25] Idem.

[26] ANITUA, Gabriel Ignacio. *Historiade lospensamientoscriminologicos.* Ciudad Autonoma de

violence .[27]

Rachel Soihet, interpreting the conclusions of Lombroso and Ferrero, states:

The normal woman, therefore, would have serious defects in proportion to those of the man, but her weak intelligence, sexual frigidity, weakness of passions, dependence, combined with maternal sentiment, kept her as a "harmless semi-criminaloid". On the other hand, those endowed with intense eroticism, with sexual sensitivity superior to that of normal women, endowed with strong intelligence, proved to be extremely dangerous; they were born criminals, whose tendencies towards evil were more numerous and varied than those of men, some born prostitutes and madwomen.[28]

For Zaffaroni, Lombroso and August Comte merely reiterated the statements already well structured by Kramer and Sprenger in The Witches' Hammer, reaffirming the total inferiority of women in relation to men.[29] Furthermore, Lombroso and Ferrero corroborated falsehood as a defining characteristic of female criminals.[30]

Still in the 19th century, Gustave Le Bonn, a racist,

Buenos Aires: Ediciones Didot, 2015. p. 60.

[27] OLIVEIRA, Marcus Vimcius Amorim de. Female crime: a phenomenon in trans-formation. In: *RevistaDialogoJurldico*, a. V, n. 5, set. 2006. p. 203-218. Available at: <http://www.ffb.edu.br/sites/default/files/dialogo_juridico_no_5.pdf>. Accessed on: October 17, 2016.

[28] SOIHET, Rachel. *Condigoes femininas e formas de violencia.* Rio de Janeiro: Forense Universitaria, 1989. p. 98.

[29] ZAFFARONI. Eugenio Raul. *La mujer y elpoderpunitivo,* op. cit.

[30] POLLAK, Otto. *The criminality of women.* op. cit, p. 9.

sexist and anti-democratic thinker, claimed that there were characteristics present in crowds that were equally present in lower forms of evolution such as women, savages and children. For Le Bonn: "Crowds are feminine everywhere, but the most feminine of all are the Latins".[31] His phrase had a double pejorative and discriminatory meaning, since in addition to criticizing the female gender, he was also talking about the inhabitants of the entire Latin American continent.[32] Le Bonn also stated that the masses were considered weak and suggestible, and therefore needed someone to manipulate them.[33] In other words, if the masses were women, then they needed someone (a man) to control them.

Corroborating Le Bonn's thinking was the Argentine doctor and positivist politician Jose Maria Ramos Mejia, who in 1899 wrote a book called *Las multitudes argentinas (The Argentine multitudes). This* author also equated the multitude with the feminine, calling it sensual and irrational, claiming that there was a danger to order and progress if the masses were to organize themselves.[34] In his ideas, Mejia went even further, as he treated the "Argentine crowd" as Indians or Spanish mestizas, bringing a strong racial component to his

---

31 LE BONN, Gustave. *Psychology of crowds.* 2. ed. Translated by Mariana Servulo da Cunha. Sao Paulo: Martins Fontes, 2016. p. 42.

32 ANITUA, Gabriel Ignacio. *Historia de lospensamientos criminologicos*, op. cit., p. 281.

33 Idem.

34. ANITUA, Gabriel Ignacio. *Historiadelospensamientoscriminologicos*. Ciudad Autonoma de Buenos Aires: Ediciones Didot, 2015. p. 283.

thinking.[35]

Between the 1930s and the 1960s, the criminologist Benigno di Tullio made not only racist but also sexist statements in his works, reintroduced from the Middle Ages, in which women were more prone to almost sinful weaknesses, including fantasy, lies, ambiguity and lust.[36] These statements corroborate the idea that women have effectively never ceased to be seen as sinful or sinful, as they were in medieval times.

Regarding the origin of the differences between genders, Engels, in his work *The Origin of the Family, Private Property and the State,* stated that with the appearance of herds and other wealth, a revolution took place in the family. It should be noted that industry and the means of production were male affairs and everything that was produced was the property of men. With the domestication of animals, however, which was also carried out by man, his wealth increased, and cattle, goods and slaves became his property alone. Women, on the other hand, only had a share in the consumption of goods, but their ownership did not belong to them. In this way, the division of labor in families had led to the distribution of property between men and women. Thus, the same cause that had ensured the supremacy of women in the home, i.e. their exclusive occupation in domestic work, now led to the preponderance of men in the home, since men's productive work was effectively

[35] Idem.

[36] Ibid, p. 371.

considered work, while domestic chores were considered merely an accessory.[37] Thus, placed inside the private space of the home, which was not even considered her own property, women were inferior to men.

Corroborating the idea outlined above, anthropologist Eleanor Leacock, based on a Marxist approach and a re-reading of Engels' work, also stated that women's subordination was related to the evolution of the idea of property. In this way, societies that were simpler and more egalitarian in terms of property and the economy would also be simpler in terms of gender.[38]

For Simone de Beauvoir, humanity would be represented by the man, so that the woman is not understood as a self-nominated being, since she always depends on the male parameter.[39] Furthermore, while the man is a thinking being without the woman, the reciprocal is not true, since the man is the one who decides what she will be and not the opposite. In this way, he is the subject, and she is just the "Other".[40] In addition, female evolution never took place, so that women only received what men agreed they should receive,[41] and even when they have abstractly recognized rights, they don't exercise them

---

[37] ENGELS, Friedrich. *The Origin of the Family, Property and the State.* Translated by Javier Bodega. 4. ed. Moscow Editorial Progreso, 2012. p. 92-93.

[38] SEGATO, Rita Laura. *The paths of genres in anthropology and beyond.* Brasilia, 1998, p. 9. Available at: <http://www.miniweb.com.br/historia/artigos/i_antiga/pdf/ serie236empdf.pdf>. Accessed on: September 8, 2016.

[39] BEAUVOIR, Simone. *The second sex* - facts and myths. 4. ed. translated by Sergio Millet. Sao Paulo: Difusao Europeia do Livro, 1970. p. 10.

[40] Idem.

[41] Ibid, p. 13.

by virtue of custom, remaining at the passive pole.[42] And partly corroborating Engels' ideas, for Beauvoir private property arose as the mistress of slaves and land, elevating men to the category of owners of women.[43] To place private property as the sole factor justifying female inferiority in society, however, would be to greatly simplify reality.[44] For the author, in addition to taking property into account as one of the factors that causes this form of inferiority, one must also consider the religious vision of Christianity, which has affirmed women as docile and pure, linked to the fragile image of the Virgin Mary.[45]

It is important to note, however, that female inferiority is the result of symbolic power, which is sneaky, as it is imposed through history, favouring the naturalization of power relations between the poles of the relationship, perpetuating this relationship which is marked by inequality. In a society marked by differentiation, the effect of universalization is one of the most powerful mechanisms through which symbolic domination is exercised, culminating in the imposition of a

---

42 Ibid, p. 14.

43 Ibid, p. 74.

44 Ibid, p. 76.

45 BARROS, Ana Maria et al. *Criminality and gender analysis:* women and crime. A study in the prison of Garanhuns - PE. p. 7. Available at: <https://www.ufpe.br/ppgdh/images/documentos/anamb3.pdf>. Accessed on: October 14, 2016.

social order.[46]

One of the forms of social differentiation is found in the division between the sexes, something considered so normal, so natural, as to be seen as inevitable.[47] The androcentric vision, however, imposes itself in such a way that it needs no justification. It is imposed in a neutral way and does not need a discourse to legitimize it, not least because the social order itself confirms the male dominance over which it is legitimized.[48] It should be noted that the masculine principle is used as a yardstick for social relations and anything that goes against it is considered wrong, not least because "the weapons of the weak are always weak weapons".[49] Thus, when the thoughts and perceptions of the dominated (in this case, women) are in accordance with the structures of the domination relationship imposed on them, their acts of knowledge are inevitably acts of recognition and sub-mission.[50]

In this way, it can be seen that women have been placed in a position of inferiority throughout history, treated as weak and unintelligent creatures, more apt to practise sin and, consequently, to be tempted into crime. It should be noted that in the 19th century, prostitution was considered the main

---

[46] BOURDIEU, Pierre. *Opodersimbolico.* Translated by Fernando Tomaz. Rio de Janeiro: Bertrand Brasil, 1989. p. 23.

[47] BOURDIEU, Pierre. *Male dominance.* 2. ed. Translated by Maria Helena Kuhner. Rio de Janeiro: Bertrand Brasil, 2002. p. 10.

[48] Ibid, p. 11.

[49] Ibid, p. 36.

[50] Ibid, p. 15.

source of infection that could lead a woman to commit crime.[51]

It should be noted that studies on women and crime only began to develop more vigorously in the 1970s, through the studies of Sandra Harding, who sought to demonstrate that modern science and a hegemonic model were based on the duality between groups: reason and emotion; subject and object; spirit and body, with the first qualities of each group belonging to the male gender, which must prevail over the second, considered feminine.[52]In this way, the paradigm of modern science aims to establish male domination by concealing gender difference, even ignoring it.[53] This explains why studies of female criminality have been forgotten for so long.

---

[51] ANITUA, Gabriel Ignacio. *Historia de lospensamientos criminologicos*, op. cit., p. 441.

[52] ARNOLD, Larissa Paim. *The effects of criminal drug policy on the profile of women selected by criminal law.* 2013. Available at: <https://www.lume.ufrgs.br/bits-tream/handle/10183/91073/000911206.pdf?sequence=1>. Accessed on: May 27, 2016.

[53] Idem.

2 WOMEN AND CRIME

As has already been explained, female inferiority has been propagated for a long time, so that this situation has also reached the issue of crime, since even the penal system, laws and criminal enforcement were created from an androgynous parameter, and currently still gravitate around men,[54] in the strict sense of the word, often causing female crime to be forgotten, forming part of the so-called black cipher.

This issue has also been addressed by Otto Pollak, who states that female criminality is a neglected field of research because the idea of a criminal is that of a man who breaks the law, since criminological research has largely adopted this cultural stereotype.[55] It should be noted that the current legal model is the result of a long historical process[56] and, as much as the lack of importance given to women in relation to criminal practice is criticized, most legal scholars prefer that the issue is not debated, generating a prejudice that, without discussion, will hardly be combated. Thus, yet another dogma is established and rarely overturned, due to the lack of criticism and discussion, which ensures the hegemony of the

---

54 BUGLIONE, Samantha. The feminine face of criminal execution. In: *Direitoe Justiga,* Revista da Faculdade de *Direito* da Pontificia Universidade Catolica do Rio Grande do Sul, v. 19, a. XX, 1998. Available at: <https://jus.com.br/artigos/946/a-mulher-enquanto-metafora- -do-direito-penal/1>. Accessed on: June 21, 2016.

55 POLLAK, Otto. *The criminality of women.* op. cit, p. XV.

56 BUGLIONE, Samantha. *The female face of penal execution.* op. cit.

ruling class.[57]

It should be noted that the majority of legal operators still have the view that crimes committed by women are generally linked to their physiological state and that such crimes are committed in more restricted, private places, since public places are still male-dominated.[58] Thus, female criminality would be reduced to gender crimes, for example, homicide by passion, infanticide, abortion, exposing or abandoning a newborn baby to hide dishonor, adultery,[59] theft. In addition to these criminal acts, women are only destined to commit other crimes related to their husbands and partners, in which they appear as accomplices,[60] with the male presence constituting a driving factor for women's entry into the world of crime.[61] In this way, female criminality is still little studied, given that women are still seen as inferior and rather sentimental beings, who don't even have the capacity to commit more serious and well-planned crimes, with a return to 19th

---

57 Idem.

58 DOS SANTOS, Maricy Beda Siqueira et al. On the other side of the walls: female criminality. In: *RevistaMnemosine,* v. 5, n. 2, p. 174-188, 2009. Available at: <http://www. mnemosine.com.br/ojs/index.php/mnemosine/article/view/180>. Accessed on: Feb. 11, 2016.

59 Adultery was defined as a crime in the Criminal Code of the Empire, in its article 250 et seq. It should be noted that if a married woman committed adultery, her sentence would be imprisonment with labor for one to three years, while a man would only be liable for adultery if he had a concubine who was faithful to him and kept him, in other words, a mistress whom he supported financially. BRAZIL. *Criminal Code of the Empire of Brazil of 1830.* Available at: <http:// www.planalto.gov.br/ccivil_03/leis/LIM/LIM-16-12-1830.htm>. Accessed on: October 18, 2016.

60 BUGLIONE, Samantha. *The female face of penal execution.* op. cit.

61 NOVAES, Elizabete David; MURARI, Ana Paula. A theoretical reflection on the inclusion of women in crime. In: *Revista Sociologia Juridica,* n. 10, jan./jun. 2010 Available at: <https://sociologiajuridicadotnet.wordpress.com/uma-reflexao-teorico-sociologica-a-cerca-da-insercao-da-mulher-na-criminalidade/>. Accessed on: October 17, 2016.

century Lombrosian ideas that treated women as weak beings. Still as a remnant of the Positivist School, however, for current legal practitioners this statement does not apply to prostitutes and homosexuals, since they are more like men, being used to the streets and violence, and are more capable of committing more serious crimes, such as murder.[62] Corroborating this idea, Zaffaroni states that: "The woman criminalized for other crimes was shown as virilized or demonstrating a degenerative pathology, because the more or less 'normal' woman could not commit violent crimes".[63] It should be noted that homicide by poisoning was typically credited to "normal" women and men with homosexual tendencies, since it was not considered a violent crime.[64]

Pollak also states that female crime is largely masked,[65] because women commit crimes, but the police have no interest in investigating them (especially with regard to younger criminals, so as not to establish a social stigma for their conduct);[66] or the victims themselves don't report the existence of the crime, as is the case, for example, with prostitutes' clients.[67]What's more, the fact that in most crimes they act as

[62] DOS SANTOS, Maricy Beda Siqueira et al. *Do outro lado* dos muros*: a criminalidade feminina.* op. cit.

[63] "Women who were criminalized for other crimes were shown as virilized or demonstrating a degenerative pathology, because more or less 'normal' women could not commit violent crimes." ZAFFARONI. Eugenio Raul. *Lamujeryelpoderpunitivo.* op. cit.

[64] *Idem.*

[65] POLLAK, Otto. *The criminality of women.* op. cit, p. 5.

[66] Ibid, p. 4.

[67] Ibid, p. 1-2.

accomplices or recipients of goods means that women remain hidden and are not punished.[68] Another point mentioned by the author is that the courts treat women more leniently than men[69] and, as a result, more men are criminalized and imprisoned than women.

Factors that can lead to female criminality include unemployment, low levels of education and precarious financial conditions. It should be noted that the vast majority of women who become involved in criminal activity are breadwinners.[70] Another factor that can influence criminal activity, especially in the case of offenses such as drug trafficking and crimes against property, is the feeling that it is easy to earn money, as well as the desire to flaunt one's power over others and acquire various goods that they would not have access to through ordinary means, such as honest work.

In reality, what happens to women criminals is a real cycle of violence, which most of the time begins during childhood and adolescence, in broken families, moving on to marriage with an equally broken husband or partner. And if the woman goes on to commit a crime, this cycle is perpetuated by the police and then by prison institutions, leaving its mark

---

[68] POLLAK, Otto. *The criminality of women.* op. cit, p. 3.

[69] Ibid, p. 5.

[70] DOSSANTOS,MaricyBedaSiqueiraetal. *Outside the walls:* female criminality. op. cit.

on the woman even when she becomes a prison inmate.[71]

In this way, "being trapped" (a temporary situation) unfolds into "being trapped", denoting a permanent sense of imprisonment, linked to a strong identity reference.[72]

---

[71] SOARES, Barbara Musumeci; ILGENFRITZ, lara. *Prisoners:* life and violence behind bars. Rio de Janeiro: Garamond, 2002. p. 126.

[72] DOS SANTOS, Maricy Beda Siqueira et al. *Do outro lado* dos muros*:* acriminalidadefemi- nina. op. cit.

3 WOMEN IN PRISON IN BRAZIL

Not unlike other places in the world, the first female arrests in Brazil were for the crimes of witchcraft and prostitution.[73] In other words, women who didn't fit the profile determined by the society of the time, which saw women as a reflection of devoted mothers and subservient women, were imprisoned. It should be noted that until the first decades of the 20th century, Brazil did not have its own prisons for women to serve their sentences for crimes. And given that most of the time the "crimes" consisted of a deviation from a "normal" social standard, the correction of female rapists was entrusted to the nuns, whose purpose was to "train" the delinquents into ladies of society.[74]

Women's prisons regulated by law in Brazil only came into being in the 1940s, following the penal reform brought about by the Penal Code of 1940, as a reflection of greater equality between men and women. Thus, the first penal institution for women was created by Decree-Law No. 3.971, of December 24, 1941, located in Bangu, Rio de Janeiro, and

---

[73] DA SILVA, Iranildo Trajano. *A brief historical and legal analysis of female incarceration in Brazil.* 2014. Available at: <http://www.boletimjuridico.com.br/doutrina/ texto.asp?id=3636>. Accessed on: June 22, 2016.

[74] DOS SANTOS, Jahira Helena P.; DOS SANTOS, Ivanna Pequeno. *Prisdes:* a contribution the origin of imprisonment in Brazil. Available at: <http://www.publicadireito.com.

called the Federal District Women's Penitentiary,[75] since at that time the city of Rio de Janeiro was the capital of Brazil. The jurists of the time, however, understood that the reduction of inequalities between the two sexes and the resulting inclusion of women in the job market would result in an increase in female crime. However, although there has been an increase in the number of crimes committed by women, even today, it is clear from criminal and prison statistics that women's participation in crime is much lower than that of men.[76]

It should be noted that the Brazilian Federal Constitution of 1988, in its Article 5, I, establishes equality between men and women.[77] The special legislation itself, however, such as the Penal Code and the Penal Execution Law (Law No. 7.210/84) only deal with convicts and internees, with few provisions expressly referring to women.[78] In this way, despite the fact that the constitutional commandment guarantees equality between the genders, in reality inequality

---

75 MOTA, Joao Luciano Marques dos Santos et al. The inclusion of women in the prison system and human rights: a legal-social problem. In: *Gender and Law*. REDOR - ENCONTRO INTERNACIONAL DE REDE FEMINISTA NORTE E NORDESTE DE ESTUDOS E PESQUISAS SOBRE MULHERES E RELAÇÕES DE GENERO, 19. Available at: <http://www.editorarealize.com.br/revistas/ebook_redor/trabalhos/gt12.pdf>. Accessed on: October 1, 2016. p. 100.

76 DOS SANTOS, Maricy Beda Siqueira et al. *Dooutroladodosmuros:* a criminalidade feminina. op. cit.

77 BRAZIL. *Constitution of the Federative Republic of Brazil of October 5, 1988.* Available at: <http://www.planalto.gov.br/ccivil_03/constituicao/constituicaocompilado.htm>. Accessed on: June 21, 2016.

78 CASTILHO, Ela Wiecko V. de. Execution of custodial sentences for women - the urgency of a special regime. In: *Revista Justitia,* Sao Paulo, 64 (197), p. 37-45, July/December 2007. Available at: <http://www.justitia.com.br/revistas/w3137c.pdf>. Accessed on: Feb. 11, 2016.

already begins with the law itself, but in a subliminal way, without people realizing what is actually happening.[79]

Thus, the Brazilian penal system reveals a differential treatment between men and women, since it is still ingrained in the minds of the majority of legal operators that women, the "weaker sex", do not commit crimes, and going further, it reveals a macho view of the problem, a view that even exists in several Brazilian regions, as if crime were a "male" thing, and it seems that only men have the capacity to commit crimes.

Women, however, also commit crimes. Not to the same extent as men, but they do commit crimes. In order to portray this reality, in 2014 the National Penitentiary Department (Depen) finalized a report on the female prison situation in Brazil, which is described below.

According to Infopen data,[80] obtained up to 2014, Brazil has the 5th largest prison population in the world, behind the United States, which is in 1st place (205,400 inmates), China (103,766), Russia (53,304) and Thailand (44,751). It should be noted that there was a 567.4% increase in the female prison population between 2000 and 2014, so that by 2014 the female prison population was 37,380. In Brazil, women make up 6.7% of the total prison population, although it is important to note that in 2000 women represented 3.2% of the total prison

---

[79] Idem.

[80] BRAZIL. Depen. *Survey of penitentiary information* - Infopen women - June 2014. Available at: <http://www.justica.gov.br/noticias/estudo-traca-perfil-da-popu- lacao-penitenciaria-feminina-no-brasil/relatorio-infopen-mulheres.pdf>. Accessed on: June 21, 2016.

population. With regard to the imprisonment rate, which shows the number of women in prison for every 100,000 inhabitants, Brazil ranks 7th in the world, with a rate of 18.5 women in prison for every 100,000 inhabitants. Another point is that while the male prison population grew by 220% from 2000 to 2014, the female population quadrupled, raising concerns about these figures. According to the report, the national *ranking of* the female prison population shows the state of Sao Paulo in 1st place (14,578 inmates); Rio de Janeiro in 2nd place (4,139 inmates) and Minas Gerais in 3rd place (3,070 inmates). It should be noted that, according to the report, 3 out of every 10 women prisoners are detained without a final conviction, however, according to the report, this figure is significantly lower than the national rate of people deprived of their liberty without a conviction, which stands at 41%.

Another point to mention is that by 2014, only 7% of prisons were exclusively for women (103 establishments) and another 17% were mixed (238), demonstrating the inequality in the Brazilian prison system which favors men over women, given that 75% of prisons in Brazil, a total of 1,070, are for men.

With regard to the profile of women prisoners, the Infopen report states that 63% of women are sentenced to custodial sentences of up to 8 years, with the majority of them serving time in a closed regime (45%). This situation shows how few alternative measures to prison are being applied, with the vast majority applying custodial sentences as the only measure that can sanction the commission of crimes.

As for the age profile, 50% of incarcerated women are between 18 and 29 years old, including those who are in the economically active age group.

As for race, color or ethnicity, the report highlights that two out of every three prisoners are black, making up 68% of the Brazilian female prison population. It is important to note, however, that the study did not include brown people among the criteria,[81] knowing that, according to the National Household Sample Survey (PNAD), carried out by the Brazilian Institute of Geography and Statistics (IBGE) in 2014, 45% of the total Brazilian population declared themselves to be brown.

As for marital status, the majority of female prisoners are single (57%), given the young age group of most of the female prison population. In addition, around 3% of female prisoners are divorced and another 3% are legally separated. The large number of single, legally separated and divorced inmates can be explained by the difficulty of conducting intimate visits in prisons and also by male prejudice in not wanting to visit or maintain a relationship with a person detained in the prison system. In addition, the report highlights that 26% of inmates are in stable unions and only 9% are married.

[81] Only white, black, yellow, indigenous and other colors, races and ethnicities are listed.

With regard to level of education, 50% of the inmates have only incomplete primary education; 14% have completed primary education; 10% have incomplete secondary education; 11% have completed secondary education; 2% have incomplete higher education; 1% have completed higher education; 8% are literate without regular courses and 4% are illiterate.

There were 583 foreign female prisoners serving time in Brazil by 2014, the majority from the following countries: 99 from Bolivia, 83 from Paraguay, 47 from South Africa, 35 from Peru and 29 from Angola. It is important to note that the Brazilian state with the highest percentage of foreign prisoners is Parana (7%).

As for the crimes committed (taking into account the people who are being prosecuted or have already been convicted), 68% of the prisoners committed the crime of drug trafficking, typified in Article 33 of Law No. 11. 343/2006; 1% committed criminal association, typified in Article 287 of the Penal Code; 9% committed theft, typified in Article 157 of the Penal Code.343/2006; 1% practiced criminal association, typified in article 288 of the Penal Code; 8% practiced robbery, typified in article 157 of the Penal Code; 9% practiced theft, typified in article 155 of the Penal Code; 2% practiced receiving, typified in article 180 of the Penal Code; 7% practiced homicide, typified in article 121 of the Penal Code; 2% practiced robbery, typified in article 157, §3 of the Penal Code; 3% have some involvement with the possession or illegal carrying of weapons (respectively articles 12 and 14 of Law No. 10. 826/2003).826/2003).

As a result, it can be seen that most of Brazil's female inmates belong to the lower classes, are often below the poverty line, and because of the lack of opportunity, end up choosing crime as a quicker and easier alternative to acquiring an economic standard that they would never achieve if they continued to do honest work. Proof of this is the widespread involvement of women in crimes such as drug trafficking and counter-patrimony. They are also often driven into crime by their own husband or partner, who ends up abandoning them in the face of arrest and conviction.

4 WOMEN IN PRISON IN ARGENTINA

In Argentina, the history of women's prisons is relatively recent, since the first institution for women dates back to 1978.[82]

According to the *International Center for Prison Studies, King's College London,* in a report carried out up to 2014, Argentina had 2,839 female prisoners, which represents 4.4% of the country's total prison population,[83] following the world average, which is also 4.4%.[84] It should be noted that, according to the *World Female Imprisonment List,* in South America Argentina is in 6th place in the ranking of the female prison population, behind other countries such as Brazil (37,380), Colombia (8,482), Peru (4,396), Venezuela (3,260) and Chile

82 CELS. Ministerio Publico de la Defensa de la Nación. *Women in prison: the scope of punishment.* Buenos Aires: Siglo Veintiuno Editores, 2011. p. 43.

83 INTERNATIONAL CENTER FOR PRISON STUDIES, KING COLLEGE LONDON. *World prisonbreaf.* 2014. Available at: <http://www.prisonstudies.org/country/argentina>. Accessed on: June 23, 2016.

CORNELL LAW SCHOOL'S AVON CENTER FOR WOMEN AND JUSTICE AND INTERNATIONAL HUMAN RIGHTS CLINIC; DEFENSORIA GENERAL DE LA NACION DE LA REPUBLICA ARGENTINA; THE UNIVERSITY OF CHICAGO LAW SCHOOL INTERNATIONAL HUMAN RIGHTS CLINIC. *Women in prison in Argentina:* causes, conditions and consequences. 2013. p. 07. Available at: <http://www.mpd.gov.ar/uploads/documentos/mujeresprision.pdf>. Accessed on: June 23, 2016.

84 INSTITUTE FOR CRIMINAL POLICY RESEARCH. WORLD PRISON BREAF. *World female imprisonment list.* 2015. Available at: <http://www.prisonstudies.org/sites/default/files/resources/downloads/world_female_imprisonment_list_third_edition_0. pdf>. Accessed on: June 23, 2016.

(3,212).[85] As for the world *ranking* , Argentina is in 30th place, behind El Salvador, which has 2,952 inmates.[86] As for the imprisonment rate, which shows the number of women in prison for every 100,000 inhabitants, Argentina has 6.9 prisoners for every 100,000 inhabitants.[87]

It should be noted that between 1990 and 2012, the female prison population in Argentina grew by 193%, while in the same period the male prison population increased by 111%.[88]

It should be noted that 55.75% of women who were incarcerated in Argentina by 2012 were imprisoned for drug-related offenses. According to a report presented by the *Procuration Penitenciaria de la Nacion Argentina* (PPN) together with the *Asamblea Permanente por los Derechos Humanos* (APDH) to thc United Nations National Council, women's incarceration has increased as a result of an increase in penalties under Argentina's narcotics law, so that by 2014, seven out of every ten women had been imprisoned for drug-

[85] Idem.

[86] Idem.

[87] INTERNATIONAL CENTER FOR PRISON STUDIES, KING COLLEGE LONDON. *World prison breaf,* op cit.

[88] CORNELL LAWSCHO OL' S AVON CENTER FOR WOMEN AND JUSTICE AND INTERNATIONAL HUMAN RIGHTS CLINIC; DEFENSORIA GENERAL DE LA NACION DE LA REPUBLICA ARGENTINA; THE UNIVERSITY OF CHICAGO LAW SCHOOL INTERNATIONAL HUMAN RIGHTS CLINIC. *Mujeres en prision en Argentina:* causas, condicio- nes y consecuencias, op. cit.

related offenses, which corresponds to approximately 70% of all women who are imprisoned in the country. In addition, 16.2% of women were arrested for crimes against property and 14.2% for crimes against people.[89]

According to the *Mujeres en prision* survey carried out in 2012 by the *National Public Prosecutor's Office,* 48% of women imprisoned in Argentina are foreigners, demonstrating the strong link between women's imprisonment in the country and international drug trafficking.[90] It should be noted that out of every ten foreigners imprisoned in Argentina, nine were arrested for drug trafficking,[91] given that they work as "mules", i.e. as the last rung in the drug trafficking chain.[92] They enter Argentina with the aim of transporting drugs, but end up being arrested and sentenced for drug trafficking. With regard to foreign prisoners, 76% of the women come from other Latin American countries. The most representative nationalities are Bolivian (27%), Peruvian (25%) and Paraguayan (7%). In addition, 7% of the women arrested are of European origin and 17% belong to the other continents.[93]

It should be noted that the UN Economic and Social

---

[89] UNITED NATIONS ORGANIZATION. Economic and Social Council. *Women deprived of liberty, a look at their rights.* 2014. Available at: <http://www.un.org/ga/search/view_doc.asp?symbol=E/CN.6/2014/NGO/68&referer=/english/&Lang=S>. Accessed on: June 23, 2016.

[90] CELS. Ministerio Publico de la Defensa de la Nacion.*Mujeres enprision: los alcances del castigo.* op. cit., p. 31.

[91] Ibid, p. 29.

[92] Ibid, p. 31.

[93] CELS. Ministerio Publico de la Defensa de la Nacion. *Women in prison:* the scope of punishment. op. cit., p. 41.

Council's report shows concern, given that 55.4% of Argentine women in prison have not yet been definitively tried.[94]

According to a report by the *Procuration Penitenciaria de la Nation Argentina* (PPN), nine out of every ten women in prison in Argentina are mothers, heads of single-parent families (55.8%) and have, on average, between two and three children under the age of 18.[95]

According to the same report, 45.2% of the women working in Argentine prisons work in sewing and dressmaking workshops, and 54.8% perform labor therapy tasks, such as horticulture, gardening and other activities.[96]

The same research states that 35.1% of incarcerated women are integrated into formal education,[97] but work is an obstacle to them being able to study, since most of these women belong to the lower economic classes and need to work from an early age, which makes access to study difficult. Thus, only 2.6% of inmates have completed higher education; 3.9% have incomplete higher education! 9.10% have completed secondary education (which corresponds to Brazilian high school)! 32.5% have incomplete secondary education! 29.9% have completed primary school! 20.8% have incomplete primary school and

[94] UNITED NATIONS ORGANIZATION (UN). Economic and Social Council. *Women deprived of their liberty, a look at their rights.* op cit.

[95] ARGENTINA.*Mujeresenprisionysituation degenero*. 2012. Available at: <http://www.ppn.gov.ar/sites/default/files/Cap%C3%ADtulo%20g%C3%A9nero%20Informe%20Anual%20 2012.pdf>. Accessed on: June 23, 2016.

[96] Idem.

[97] Idem.

1.30% have no schooling.[98]

With regard to age, the same survey showed that 73.6% of inmates are women aged over 30: 41.2% are aged between 31 and 39! 32.4% are aged 40 or over and only 26.4% are aged between 18 and 29. Only 12% are over 50 years old. Thus, it can be seen that the female prison population in Argentina is older than the male population, as the majority of this prison population is between the ages of 25 and 34, which represents a percentage of 39%, corresponding to 26,755 inmates.[99]

Another fact to mention is that in the age group of 40 and over, there is a higher incidence of the crime of selling drugs. In addition, there is a higher incidence of crimes against property among women in the 18-29 age group (30.8%) and women in the 30-39 age group commit more crimes against people (21.3%).[100]

With regard to the length of the sentence, 63.5% of the women definitively convicted in Argentina serve sentences of 4 to 5 years in prison,[101] bearing in mind that the penalties for

---

98 CELS. Ministerio Publico de la Defensa de la Nacion. *Women in prison:* the scope of punishment. op. cit., p. 37.

99 ARGENTINA, Sistema Nacional de Estadisticas para la Ejecucion de las Penas (SNEEP). *Criminal Policy Statistics.* 2014. Available at: <http://www.jus.gob.ar/areas-tematicas/estadisticas-de-politica-criminal/mapa.aspx>. Accessed on: June 23, 2016.

100 CELS. Ministerio Publico de la Defensa de la Nacion. *Mujeresenprision:* los alcances del castigo. op. cit, p. 29.

101 Ibid. p. 34.

drug trafficking are 4 to 15 years in prison, according to articles 5 and 6 of Law No. 23.737/89.[102]

As for their occupation, 26% of the detainees said that before their arrest they did domestic work, 15% were *"changas"*, i.e. peddlers, selling products on the streets or at street markets, 19% worked in commerce, 13% in technical and administrative jobs, 8% in sewing workshops or factories, 16% in other jobs and 3% engaged in prostitution.[103]

Argentina, following a trend in Latin America, has the majority of women imprisoned for drug trafficking, since its poor financial situation, aggravated by the economic crisis that has plagued the country for several years, creates the illusion of economic improvement through drug trafficking.

---

102 ARGENTINA. *Ley nº23.737 de 21 de septiembre de 1989.* Available at: <http://www.ppn.gov.ar/sites/default/files/Ley%2023.737.Modificacion%20al%20C%C3%B3digo%20Penal- -Narcotr%C3%A1fico.pdf>. Accessed on: June 24, 2016.

103 CELS. Ministerio Publico de la Defensa de la Nacion. *Mujeresenprision:* los alcances del castigo. op. cit, p. 38.

5 FINAL CONSIDERATIONS

As demonstrated throughout this work, women have always been accompanied by a stigma of inferiority. For a long time, female criminality was restricted to prostitutes and homosexuals, since they were similar to men. In other words, it was as if the "normal" woman, a weak and inferior being, didn't have the capacity to plan a crime, and that this was an attribute only of men, who were intelligent and cunning. Thus, criminology, criminalistics and criminal law itself did not debate the issue of female criminality, because if women don't commit crimes, why should we debate that they don't exist?

Thus, it was only in the 1970s that studies began into this type of crime, trying to profile the women who are most likely to commit offenses. With this in mind, most countries have undertaken studies to discover the reasons why women become involved in crime.

With regard to the comparison between the total female population and the female incarcerated population in Brazil and Argentina, we have the following data: the total female population in Brazil, according to IBGE data up to 2013, was 103,500,000 women, which corresponded to 51.4% of the country's total population. As for the female prison population, according to Infopen data, by 2014, Brazil had 37,380 women in prison, which corresponded to 0.036% of the total female population. In Argentina, according to data from datamacro.com, the total female population was 21,951,000 in 2014, which corresponded to 51.07% of the country's total population. As for the female prison population, there were a total of 2,839 incarcerated women, which corresponded to 0.012% of the country's total population.

As for the profile of women held in the Brazilian prison system until 2014, Infopen reported that Brazil has the 5th largest female prison population in the world and that there has been a worrying growth of over 500% in the period between 2000 and 2014. In addition, women represent 6.7% of the total prison population, yet only 7% of prisons are exclusively for women, so that there is a predominance of male and mixed prisons. With regard to the sentences handed down, there is a predominance of custodial sentences, as 63% of women's sentences are for around 8 years, which makes it difficult to apply benefits such as conditional suspension of sentences and the substitution of custodial sentences for restrictive sentences. As for the age of the women in prison, 50% of them are between 18 and 29 years old, which is in line with the male age group in prison, which is just as young, since 56% of the men in prison are in the same age group. In addition, the vast majority of inmates are single (56%), have only incomplete primary education (50%), and most of them (68%) are in prison for drug trafficking. With regard to foreign inmates, the number is quite small, as by 2014 there were only 583 women, out of a total female prison population of 37,380, representing only 1.55% of the women imprisoned in Brazil.

As for Argentina, according to a report by the *International Center for Prison Studies, King's College London, the* country has 2,839 female inmates, which translates into 4.4% of the country's total prison population, and is only 30th in the world *ranking of* the female prison population. It should be noted that between 1990 and 2012, the population grew by around 193%. The number of women imprisoned in Argentina reflects a worldwide trend in which drug trafficking is the main criminal factor that leads to the imprisonment of so many women, as 55.75% of them are imprisoned for this crime. Contrary to what happens in Brazil, where the population of foreign female prisoners is tiny, in Argentina they represent 48% of all women in prison. This is due to international drug trafficking, which compels them to leave their countries in an attempt to make a high and easy profit. As in Brazil, the majority of foreign women in Argentina are Latin American and mainly of Bolivian origin. Unlike Brazil, however, where the majority of female prisoners have only incomplete primary education (50%), in Argentina 29.9% of them have completed primary education, demonstrating a better level of schooling in that country.

parents. With regard to the age of female prisoners, it can be seen that in Argentina most of them are over 30 years old (73.6%). This differs from the percentage of men in prison, since

39% of men in prison in Argentina are aged between 25 and 34.

Thus, the most striking points in the analysis of women in prison in the two countries are the following: the population of female prisoners in both countries follows the global trend of female incarceration due to drug trafficking, which leads these women, who are often heads of single-parent families, to enter the world of crime, not only with the intention of showing off their wealth and possessions, but also to provide a better socio-economic condition for their children, since the system itself makes it difficult for them to be included. It should be noted that while in Brazil the female prison population is quite young (50% of them are between 18 and 29 years old), in Argentina 76.3% of inmates are over 30 years old. These percentages are reflected in their level of schooling and in their ability to work, because being younger, there is an indication that the inmates started committing criminal offenses at an early age, and it can be said that they have not studied or worked much. Another interesting point concerns the number of foreign prisoners in Argentina for drug trafficking, which shows that this country is on an international trafficking route, something that could lead to greater restrictions on the entry of people considered suspicious, especially women, given the large number of foreign prisoners.

In this context, there are different points between the faces of female incarceration in Brazil and Argentina. One thing that is quite evident, however, is that the female prison population is increasing considerably in both countries, something that is of great concern, since it is necessary to analyze the social structure of both countries in order to understand why so many women are turning to crime, and to find solutions to prevent the high incarceration rates from continuing to rise.

6 REFERENCES

ANITUA, Gabriel Ignacio. *History of criminological thinking.* Ciudad Autonoma de Buenos Aires: Ediciones Didot, 2015.

ARGENTINA. *Law No. 23.737 of September 21, 1989.* Available at: <http://www.ppn.gov.ar/sites/default/files/Ley%2023.737.Modificacion%20 al%20C%C3%B3digo%20Penal-Narcotr%C3%A1fico.pdf>. Accessed on: June 24, 2016.

. Sistema Nacional de Estadisticas para la Ejecucion de las Penas (SNEEP). *Criminal Policy Statistics.* 2014. Available at: <http:// www.jus.gob.ar/areas-tematicas/estadisticas-de-politica-criminal/mapa.aspx>. Accessed on: June 23, 2016.

ARGENTINA. PROCURACION PENITENCIARIA DE LA NACION. *Mujeres enprisiony situation degenero.* 2012. Available at: <http://www.ppn.gov.ar/ sites/default/files/Cap%C3%ADtulo%20g%C3%A9nero%20Informe%20Anual%20 2012.pdf>. Accessed on: June 23, 2016.

ARNOLD, Larissa Paim. *The effects of criminal drug policy on the profile of women selected by criminal law.* 2013. Available at: <https://www. lume.ufrgs.br/bitstream/handle/10183/91073/000911206.pdf?sequence=1>.
Accessed on: May 27, 2016.

BARROS, Ana Maria et al. *Criminality and gender analysis:*

women and crime. A study in the Garanhuns - PE penitentiary. p. 7. Available at: <https://www.ufpe.br/ppgdh/images/documentos/anamb3.pdf>. Accessed on: October 14, 2016.

BEAUVOIR, Simone de. *The second sex* - facts and myths. 4. ed. Translated by Sergio Millet. Sao Paulo: Difusao Europeia do Livro, 1970.

BOURDIEU, Pierre. *Male domination. 2.* ed. Translated by Maria Helena Kuhner. Rio de Janeiro: Bertrand Brasil, 2002.

. *Opodersimbolico.* Translated by Fernando Tomaz. Rio de Janeiro: Bertrand Brasil, 1989.

BRAZIL. *Criminal Code of the Empire of Brazil of 1830.* Available at: <http://www.planalto.gov.br/ccivil_03/leis/LIM/LIM-16-12-1830.htm>. Accessed on: October 18, 2016.

. *Constitution of the Federative Republic of Brazil of October 5, 1988.* Available at:<http://www.planalto.gov.br/ccivil_03/constituicao/constituicaocompilado.htm>. Accessed on: June 21, 2016.

. Depen. *Survey of penitentiary information* - Infopen women - June 2014. Available at:< http://www.justica.gov.br/noticias/estudo-traca-perfil-da-populacao-penitenciaria-feminina-no-brasil/relatorio- -infopen-mulheres.pdf>. Accessed on: June 21,

2016.

BUENODOMINGUEZ, MariaLuisa. Labrujeriados maleficioscontra los hombres. In: *Clioy Crimen,* n. 08, p. 125-142, 2011. Available at: <https:// www.durango-udala.net/portalDurango/RecursosWeb/DOCUMEN- TOS/1/1_5142_3.pdf>. Accessed on: September 29, 2015.

BUGLIONE, Samantha. The feminine face of penal execution. In : *Direito e Jus- tiqa*, Revista da Faculdade de Direito da Pontificia Universidade Catolica do Rio Grande do Sul, v. 19, a. XX, 1998. Available at: <https://jus.com.br/ artigos/946/a-mulher-enquanto-metafora-do-direito-penal/1>. Accessed on: June 21, 2016.

CASTILHO, Ela Wiecko V. de. Execution of custodial sentences for women - the urgency of a special regime. In: *Revista Justitia*, Sao Paulo, 64 (197), p. 37-45, July/December 2007. Available at: <http://www.justitia. com.br/revistas/w3137c.pdf>. Accessed on: Feb. 11, 2016.

CELS. Ministerio Publico de la Defensa de la Nación. *Women in prison:* the scope of punishment. Buenos Aires: Siglo Veintiuno Editores, 2011.

CORNELL LAW SCHOOL'S AVON CENTER FOR WOMEN AND JUSTICE AND INTERNATIONAL HUMAN RIGHTS CLINIC; DEFENSORIA GENERAL DE LA NACION DE LA

REPUBLICAARGENTINA; THE UNIVERSITY OF CHICAGO LAW SCHOOL INTERNATIONAL HUMAN RIGHTS CLINIC. *Women in prison in Argentina:* causes, conditions and consequences. 2013. p. 7. Available at: <http://www.mpd.gov.ar/uploads/documentos/mujeres-prision.pdf>. Accessed on: June 23, 2016.

COULANGES, Fustel de. *The Ancient City* - Studies in the Cult, Law and Institutes of Greece and Rome. 12. ed. Translated by Jonas Camargo Leite and Eduardo Fonseca. Sao Paulo: Hemus, 1975.

DA SILVA, Iranildo Trajano. *A brief historical and legal analysis of female imprisonment in Brazil.* 2014. Available at: <http://www.boletimjuri-dico.com.br/doutrina/texto.asp?id=3636>. Accessed on: June 22, 2016.

DOS SANTOS, Jahira Helena P.; DOS SANTOS, Ivanna Pequeno. *Prisons:* an account of the origins of incarceration in Brazil. Available at:<http:// www.publicadireito.com.br/artigos/?cod=c76fe1d8e0846243>. Accessed on: June 22, 2016.

DOS SANTOS, Maricy Beda Siqueira et al. On the other side of the walls: female criminality. In: *RevistaMnemosine,* vol. 5, n.

2, p. 174-188, 2009. Available at: <http://www.mnemosine.com.br/ojs/index.php/mnemosine/ article/view/180>. Accessed on: 11feb. 2016.

ENGELS, Friedrich. *The Origin of the Family, Property and the State*. 4. ed. Moscow: Editorial Progreso, 1981.

. *The origins of the family, property and the State*. Translated by Javier Bodega. 4. ed. Moscow: Editorial Progreso, 2012.

INTERNATIONAL CENTER FOR PRISON STUDIES, KING COLLEGE LONDON. *Worldprisonbreaf*. 2014. Available at:<http://www.prisonstu- dies.org/country/argentina>. Accessed on: June 23, 2016.

INSTITUTE FOR CRIMINAL POLICY RESEARCH. WORLD PRISON BREAF. *Worldfemale imprisonment list*. 2015. Available at: <http://www.prisonstu- dies.org/sites/default/files/resources/downloads/world_female_i mprison- ment_list_third_edition_0.pdf>. Accessed on: June 23, 2016.

KRAMER, Heinrich; SPRENGER, Jacobus. *MalleusMaleficarum*. Translated by Floreal Maza. [s.l.]: Ediciones Orion, 1486.

LE BONN, Gustave. *Psychology of crowds*. 2. ed. Translation Mariana Servulo da Cunha. Sao Paulo: Martins Fontes, 2016.

LOBATO, Aline, et al. *Women criminals:* analyzing the

relationship between family breakdown and criminality. p.3. Available at: <http://www.abrapso. org. br/siteprincipal/images/Anais_XVENABRAPSO/242.%20mulheres%20 criminosas.pdf>. Accessed on: October 14, 2016.

LOMBROSO, Cesare; FERRERO, William. *The Female Offender*. New York: D. Appleton Company, 1898.

MOTA, Joao Luciano Marques dos Santos et al. The inclusion of women in the prison system and human rights: a legal-social problem. In: *Gender and Law*. REDOR - ENCONTRO INTERNACIONAL DE REDE FEMINISTA NORTE E NORDESTE DE ESTUDOS E PESQUISAS SOBRE MULHERES E RELAÇÕES DE GENERO, 19. Available at: <http://www. editorarealize.com.br/revistas/ebook_redor/trabalhos/gt12.pdf>. Accessed on: October 1, 2016.

NOVAES, Elizabete David; MURARI, Ana Paula. A theoretical reflection on the inclusion of women in crime. In: *RevistaSociologiaJuridica,n.10,* jan./jun. 2010. Available at: <https://sociologiajuridicadotnet.wordpress. com/uma-reflexao-teorico-sociologica-acerca-da-insercao-da-mulher-na-criminalidade/>. Accessed on: October 17, 2016.

OLIVEIRA, Marcus Vinicius Amorim de. Criminality feminine: a phenomenon in transformation. In: *Revista Dialogo Juridico,* a. V, n. 5, set. 2006.

p. 203-218. Available at: <http://www.ffb.edu.br/sites/default/files/dia-logo_juridico_no_5.pdf>. Accessed on: October 17, 2016.

UNITED NATIONS ORGANIZATION (UN). Economic and Social Council. *Mujeres privadas de libertad, una mirada sobre sus derechos.* 2014. Available at: <http://www.un.org/ga/search/view_doc.asp7symboUE/CN.6/2014/NGO/68&referer=/english/&Lang=S>. Accessed on: June 23, 2016.

PIRE S, JoaoD avi Avelar. The inquisition and witchcraft: an aritualization of interrogation and torture. In: *RevistaHistoriae Cultura,* Franca, SP, v. 2, n. 3 (especial), p. 560-573, 2013. Available at: <http://periodicos.franca.unesp.br/index.php/historiaecultura/article/view/1121>. Accessed on: September 29, 2015.

POLLAK, Otto. *The criminality of women.* New York: Perpetua Books, 1961.

SEGATO, Rita Laura. *The paths of genres in anthropology and beyond.* Brasilia, 1998, p. 9. Available at: <http://www.miniweb.com.br/histo-ria/artigos/i_antiga/pdf/serie236empdf.pdf>. Accessed on: September 8, 2016.

SOARES, Barbara Musumeci; ILGENFRITZ, lara. *Prisoners:* life and violence behind bars. Rio de Janeiro: Garamond, 2002.

SOIHET, Rachel. *Feminine conditions and forms of violence.* Rio de Janeiro: Forense Universitaria, 1989.

ZAFFARONI, Eugenio Raul. *Women and punitive power*. 1992. Available at: <http://www.cubc.mx/biblioteca/libros/Zaffaroni%20-%20Mujer%20y%20 poder%20punitivo.pdf>. Accessed on: September 28, 2015.

INDICE

MIX
Papier aus verantwortungsvollen Quellen
Paper from responsible sources
FSC® C105338

Printed by Books on Demand GmbH, Norderstedt / Germany